SPACE UNIVERSITY™

THE SPACE EXPLORER'S GUIDE TO

Out-of-this-World Science

BY
HENA KHAN

WITH
MARIANNE DYSON
TECHNICAL CONSULTANT

MINNA PALAQUIBAY
SPACE EDUCATOR

RYAN WYATT
VISUAL ADVISOR

AND
JIM SWEITZER, PH.D.
NASA SCIENCE CENTER,
DePAUL UNIVERSITY

SCHOLASTIC INC.

NEW YORK   TORONTO   LONDON   AUCKLAND   SYDNEY
MEXICO CITY   NEW DELHI   HONG KONG   BUENOS AIRES

Who's Who at Space U.

Hena Khan
Writer
Hena is a writer who lives in Maryland. She has written three books for Space University and is fascinated by science in orbit.

Marianne Dyson
Consultant
Marianne is a former NASA mission controller and award-winning nonfiction author who dreams of touring the galaxy.

Ryan Wyatt
Visual Advisor
Ryan designs scientific visuals for the American Museum of Natural History's Rose Center for Earth and Space.

Minna Palaquibay
Consultant
Minna designs and teaches science programs for kids at the American Museum of Natural History's Rose Center for Earth and Space.

Jim Sweitzer
Advisor
Jim is an astrophysicist and the director of the NASA Space Science Center at DePaul University in Chicago.

ISBN: 0-439-55747-X

Copyright © 2004 by Scholastic Inc.

Editor: Andrea Menotti
Assistant Editor: Megan Gendell
Designers: Diana Fitter, Peggy Gardner, Lee Kaplan, Tricia Kleinot
Illustrators: Yancey C. Labat, Ed Shems

Photos:
Front cover: The Destiny Lab Module of the International Space Station (image by NASA)
Back cover: The International Space Station over the Earth (image by NASA)
Title page: Salt crystals and a plant grown in space (images by NASA)

All photos by NASA unless noted below.
Page 9: Sheila Terry/Photo Researchers. Page 14: (potatoes) Wisconsin Center for Space Automation and Robotics at the University of Wisconsin. Page 16: (rice and peppers) Susan Frantz. Pages 22, 23, and 48: (fish) Dr. Kenichi Ijiri. Pages 24 and 48: (ants) Spacehab. Page 24: (spiderweb) Dr. Jeremy Burgess/Photo Researchers. Page 27: (NEEMO): NOAA's Undersea Research Center at the University of North Carolina at Wilmington. Page 46: Fisher Space Pen Company.

12 11 10 9 8 7 6 5 4 3 2 1   4 5 6 7 8 9/0

Printed in the U.S.A.

First Scholastic printing, June 2004

The publisher has made every effort to ensure that the activities in this book are safe when done as instructed. Adults should provide guidance and supervision whenever the activity requires.

Table of Contents

SCIENCE

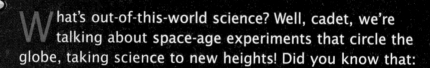

hat's out-of-this-world science? Well, cadet, we're talking about **space-age experiments that circle the** globe, taking science to new heights! Did you know that:

- A rose will smell different in space than on Earth?

- Crystals grown in space are bigger and more perfect than those grown on Earth?

- Ants, spiders, jellyfish, snails, and newts have all been sent up into space?

- Wheat, potatoes, soybeans, and flowers have all been grown in space?

- Space-sick fish swim round and round in circles?

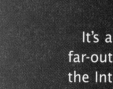

- Rats cling to each other in space because they hate being weightless?

- Kids like you have grown plants using seeds that spent time in space?

It's all true! This month, Space University **is bringing you a glimpse of the** far-out finds that astronaut-scientists bring **back to Earth from spacecraft like** the International Space Station (ISS). Plus, **you'll get to try out some space-style** experiments for yourself!

Like You've Never Never Seen It!

HOW IS SCIENCE IN SPACE DIFFERENT FROM SCIENCE ON EARTH?

Well, for starters, when scientists do experiments onboard a spacecraft, they have a little thing called weightlessness to deal with—where things don't fall down and there's no right side up! Plus, out in space there's no air, and temperatures get super hot in direct sunlight and freezing cold in the shade. Not only that, but the spacecraft also gets hit with radiation from the Sun and cosmic rays from deep space!

WHY IS IT SO IMPORTANT TO DO SCIENCE IN SPACE?

Take a guess, cadet! Is it because:

A) Studying the ways things work and behave in space will help us figure out how to live and travel out there longer?

B) We might be able to find new medicines and gain a better understanding of how our bodies work?

C) Space science can lead to the development of all sorts of cool gadgets, equipment, and lifesaving technology?

Hmmm...trick question? You bet, cadet! Space science is important for *all* of those reasons, and a whole lot more! With all the differences in the space environment, it's hard to know how humans, plants, animals, and other Earthling stuff will behave up there. That's why we do experiments in space: to help us understand the changes that happen to things while they're in space so we can prevent them, fix them, or use them to work for us somehow.

The world has a lot riding on what scientists learn in space, and you're about to find out about the amazing stuff that goes on out there. Ready to see science like you've never seen it before? Then grab your lab coat and Space Case and prepare for liftoff!

WHAT'S IN THIS MONTH'S SPACE CASE?

This month, your Space Case is full of the stuff you need to try some out-of-this-world science yourself—without leaving the planet! You've got:

- **A magnifier with a light.** Give your eyeballs a boost with your new Space U magnifier! Insert the batteries and then use your magnifier to look at your own plant sprouts and crystals!

- **A packet of radish seeds.** These little seeds will give you a glimpse into the world of space plants. Hop over to page 17 to get *growing*!

- **Epsom salts and a string.** Epsom salts might be good for soaking sore feet, but did you know you can also make crystals with them? You sure can! Turn to page 35 to start creating cosmically cool crystals!

THE SPACE UNIVERSITY WEB SITE

Scientists are always sharing and comparing their results with other scientists—and that's just what you can do on this month's Space U web site (www.scholastic.com/space)! Visit the bulletin board to post your experiment results and see what other cadets discovered! And just like every month, you'll find two great new web missions for more out-of-this-world fun. Stop by the site soon!

Complete this month's web missions to earn your personalized mission patch. Then you can paste it right here!

PLANET PASSWORD

This month's web site password is:

SPACELAB

As you might imagine, the biggest change when science goes up into space is that everything's weightless. Is that because there's no gravity up there? No way, Cadet José! If this comes as a surprise, then check out *The Space Explorer's Guide to Space Travel*, where you'll find the whole story of weightlessness in space. Or, read on for the quick version!

WAIT—WHY WEIGHTLESSNESS?

The force of gravity *does* decrease as you move away from Earth, but when you're orbiting in a spacecraft, you're only about 200 miles (320 km) above the surface—not very far. If you were standing on top of a really tall tower 200 miles above the Earth, the force of gravity would be only a little less than what you feel on the surface. If you stood on a scale on the top of that tower, you'd weigh just 9 percent less than what you weigh right now.

So how does weightlessness happen? Well, if you stepped off that 200-mile-high tower (yikes!), you'd be pulled down in a straight line by gravity. While you were falling, you'd be in *free fall* and would be weightless—until you hit the ground (double yikes!).

If you took a running *leap* from the tower, you'd still be pulled down, but you'd land a good distance away from the base of the tower. If you climbed into a *cannon* and launched yourself off the tower going 17,500 miles per hour (28,000 km/h), you'd fly past the horizon and *never* hit the ground. The Earth's gravity would pull you into a circle, or orbit, around the planet. And as long as you stayed in orbit, you'd still be in free fall, just like before, and you'd stay weightless.

So that's how weightlessness works! Now, the question is: How do scientists study the *effects* of weightlessness and other aspects of the space environment? By carefully setting up experiments using the *scientific method*, as you'll learn on the next page!

WHERE IN THE WORLD DO I BEGIN?

So how do you go about doing an experiment in space? Well, just like on Earth, you use the *scientific method*.

With the scientific method, you start out with a question you want to answer, like, "What will happen if I change the channel while my sister is watching her favorite show?"

Next, you form a *hypothesis*, which is a prediction of what will happen, like, "My sister will scream." The next step is to design an *experiment* to test whether your hypothesis is true or false. That's the tricky part—you have to make sure that your experiment is testing exactly what you want to find out (and that something else isn't affecting your results!). For example, if you not only changed the channel but *also* grabbed your sister's bag of potato chips and kicked her off the couch, you wouldn't know if changing the channel was what made your sis scream, or if it was something else. That's why scientists are careful to design experiments that test only one *variable* (or change) at a time.

Lab Lingo

Hypothesis: A prediction based on prior knowledge or observations.

Experiment: A test of a hypothesis in which a scientist changes a certain variable and observes the effects.

Procedure: A series of steps that are followed to complete an experiment.

Variable: Anything you change in an experiment that might affect the outcome.

Control: A version of an experiment in which no changes are made. The "control" is then compared to versions of the same experiment in which a variable is changed.

Observation: The information (or data) collected using your five senses as you perform your experiment.

Conclusion: A final summing up of the results of an experiment.

BY GEORGE, I THINK I'VE GOT IT!

During an experiment, a scientist carefully records detailed observations, measurements, and notes. Once all the data is collected, it's time to form a conclusion and share it with others. Other scientists can then repeat the experiment to see if they get the same results.

LOGBOOK LOGIC

Good scientists, whether they work in space or on the ground, keep a logbook for each experiment they do—and so should you! Get a notebook and label it "Experiment Logbook." Use it to keep track of your procedures, observations, and discoveries. Make sure you include the following:

- **Your hypothesis**
- **Date (or dates)** when you conducted the experiment
- **Your procedure**
- **Your observations** (including drawings or photos!)
- **Your conclusions**

This way, you'll have records of all your hard work, and you'll be able to refer to your notes in the future, in case you decide to do a follow-up experiment or share your results with others.

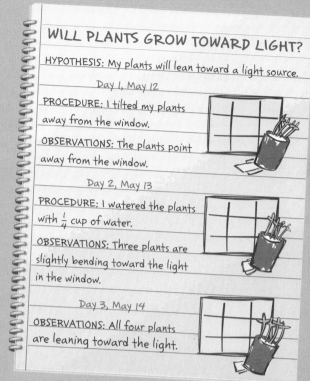

WILL PLANTS GROW TOWARD LIGHT?

HYPOTHESIS: My plants will lean toward a light source.

Day 1, May 12

PROCEDURE: I tilted my plants away from the window.

OBSERVATIONS: The plants point away from the window.

Day 2, May 13

PROCEDURE: I watered the plants with $\frac{1}{4}$ cup of water.

OBSERVATIONS: Three plants are slightly bending toward the light in the window.

Day 3, May 14

OBSERVATIONS: All four plants are leaning toward the light.

✱Astrotales

Galileo: The Father of Modern Science

Galileo Galilei
(1564–1642)

By now, you've probably heard the name Galileo Galilei thrown around Space University a few times. That's because he made amazing discoveries about our solar system that forever changed the way people looked at the universe and our place in it. But Galileo is also known as the "father of modern science." What did an Italian guy born back in the 1500s do to earn a whopper of a title like that?

Well, back in Galileo's day, the accepted thing to do if you wondered about something was to study history and find out what the ancient philosophers had to say about it. For example, back then scholars wondered whether something flying through the air would get hotter or colder. To find out, a scholar named Orazio Grassi did some research and found a Greek historian claiming that people in ancient Babylon (in the Middle East) cooked raw eggs by putting them in slings and swinging them in circles. So Grassi concluded that spinning something through the air must make it heat up.

Does that convince you? Probably not! Back then, however, this was a perfectly acceptable way of answering a scientific question. But not for Galileo!

Galileo wanted to see for himself what would happen if he spun an egg in circles. He actually put a raw egg in a sling and swung it around and around and around until—that's right, nothing happened to it! He ended up with a raw egg and a tired arm.

Galileo concluded that spinning the egg didn't cook it or heat it up. In fact, he discovered that if you start out with a hot egg and spin it, it will cool! Galileo wrote up his conclusions, making fun of Grassi while he was at it.

Since Galileo believed in testing things for himself, he's credited with being the first person to develop an experiment-based approach to science—commonly known as the scientific method. You know the method and its steps, which include predictions (or hypotheses), procedures, observations, and conclusions. That's the way science has been done ever since! It all makes a lot of sense—so much so that you probably can't imagine it any other way, right?

CATCH SOME RAYS

One important aspect of the space environment that scientists need to study and understand is the Sun's radiation. How does it affect spacecraft, satellites, and, of course, *people* that are sent into space? See what you can discover about the power of the Sun's rays!

Launch Objective

> **Get familiar with the scientific method by studying the effects of radiation exposure (in the form of sunlight) on paper.**

Your equipment

- **Logbook and pencil**
- **Fresh newspaper**
- **Scissors**
- **Three plastic bags with zip closures**
- **Brown paper bag**
- **Two paper clips**
- **Rock or paperweight**
- **Sunscreen**

Mission Procedure

1 Predict what will happen to newspaper that is unprotected from the Sun's radiation compared to newspaper that is protected. This is your hypothesis—write it down in your logbook.

2 Cut out three small square pieces of newspaper (use the classified page, if you have it, so the pieces are nearly identical).

3 Place the newspaper cuttings into the plastic bags and seal them shut.

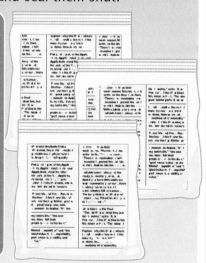

4 Put one bag inside the brown paper bag. This is your control—the paper that won't be exposed to any sunlight. You'll compare this one to the others at the end of the experiment.

5 Find a sunny spot outside for your bags.

6 Set down the brown paper bag and attach the other two plastic bags to the outside with paper clips. Put a rock or paperweight on the bag so it doesn't blow away!

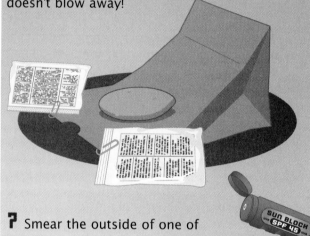

7 Smear the outside of one of the paper-clipped bags with sunscreen.

8 Record the date and time in your logbook.

9 Check back every hour to be sure the bag hasn't been disturbed or covered by shade. If the sky gets cloudy for more than an hour, bring the bag inside, record the time it was outside, and try again the next sunny day. Try to get at least twelve hours total of full Sun exposure before ending the experiment.

10 What do you notice about all of the newspaper pieces? Did any of them change color? Which changed the most? Did the sunscreen protect the paper from the Sun? Record your results in your logbook!

Science, Please!

In this experiment, you were trying to find out the effects of exposure to radiation (in the form of sunlight) on newspaper. You might have hypothesized that "exposure to sunlight for at least one day will make newspaper a different color than paper kept in the dark"—and you would've been right!

The *variable* in your experiment was sunlight—each bag got a different amount of it. But to have a really good experiment, you needed to make sure that other variables didn't change. For example, you wouldn't want the amount of moisture to be different in each case—then you wouldn't know if your newspaper changed because of moisture or because of sunlight! That's why you put all your newspaper pieces in plastic bags to keep them dry.

You should have observed that the newspaper with no sunscreen turned the most yellow from the sunlight. This is because bright sunlight causes a chemical reaction in paper that makes light-colored paper darken. The newspaper in the paper bag shouldn't have changed color since it was shielded from the Sun. The newspaper with sunscreen should have changed color less, if at all.

More From Mission Control

Now that you've seen how newspaper responds to radiation, try seeing how other types of paper (like magazine pages or notebook paper) respond. Some paper has been treated with a coating so that sunlight won't damage it as much. What kind of paper seems to hold up the best under the Sun?

You can also try putting *dark* paper out in the Sun to see what happens to it. Or try drawing lines with markers and see if different colors respond differently to the Sun's radiation! Write out a hypothesis for each variable you think of, design an experiment to test it, and keep track of all your observations and discoveries in your logbook!

✴Astrotales

A Different Kind of Space Case

If radiation can change the color of paper on Earth, imagine what it can do to things in space—where there's no atmosphere for protection! What would happen to papers, paints, or even metals?

Scientists set out to study that very question through the Materials International Space Station Experiment (MISSE), which was designed to see how over 900 different materials would hold up in space. In this experiment, a suitcase-sized container held trays filled with samples ranging from paint to solar cells. The open container was attached to the outside of the ISS and left to face the space environment for anywhere from one to three years at a time. The samples were then returned to Earth, where they were analyzed by researchers seeking to develop long-lasting materials for spacecraft, satellites, and even your home on Earth!

◄ Here's one of the trays of samples that MISSE took into space.

Welcome to SPACELAB!

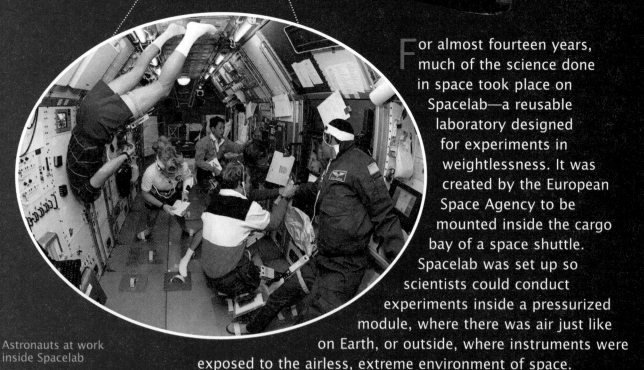

In this drawing you can see where Spacelab was placed inside a space shuttle's cargo bay.

Astronauts floated from the shuttle's cabin to the lab using this passageway.

Astronauts at work inside Spacelab

For almost fourteen years, much of the science done in space took place on Spacelab—a reusable laboratory designed for experiments in weightlessness. It was created by the European Space Agency to be mounted inside the cargo bay of a space shuttle. Spacelab was set up so scientists could conduct experiments inside a pressurized module, where there was air just like on Earth, or outside, where instruments were exposed to the airless, extreme environment of space.

On Spacelab, astronauts performed experiments ranging from making crystals to growing potatoes. They tested the effects of weightlessness on stuff like liquids and on creatures like rats, monkeys, frogs, fruit flies, and jellyfish! Many missions were flown before Spacelab was retired so NASA could focus its attention on science on the International Space Station.

SCIENCE on the ISS

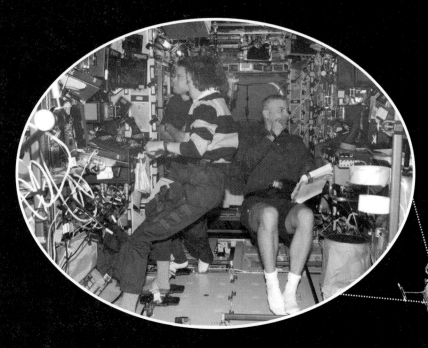

Astronauts working in the Destiny Lab

Now, space science is taking place every day, twenty-four hours a day, on the ISS. There is currently one permanent laboratory module in place on the ISS: the Destiny Lab Module. There are plans to add two more lab modules in the years to come—a Japanese module and a European module. The advantage of science on the ISS is that experiments aren't limited to the duration of the shuttle flights (about two weeks), like they were on Spacelab.

Part 2: Plants in Space

How would you like to eat a strawberry that was grown in space? Do you think it would look, feel, and taste the same as one grown on Earth? Well, scientists are answering those very questions by sending plants and seeds into space and watching how they grow and adapt in weightlessness.

A plant grown aboard the ISS, with water droplets clinging to its leaves

Plants in space have to deal with different conditions than they're used to on Earth, like less room to grow—there's no room for a field of corn onboard the ISS! Scientists also worry about the effects of radiation and the air quality onboard a spacecraft. With all these changes, scientists want to test whether plants will grow normally over years and years in space.

These little potatoes were successfully grown in space! They grew onboard a space shuttle using special equipment designed at the University of Wisconsin.

Why worry about growing stuff in space? Well, for now the only food astronauts eat in space is the stuff that's brought up from Earth. The goal is for astronauts to be able to grow their own food someday. That would make long-term space living easier, and it would make long-distance space travel to faraway places like Mars more likely.

Apart from food, plants could also be used to produce oxygen for astronauts to breathe, since all plants convert carbon dioxide into oxygen through the process of photosynthesis. Research has also shown that plants and their roots can clean air and water of pollutants. Plus, you never know, maybe in space you could grow better-tasting, more nutritious food than on Earth. One day you could be chomping on space imports!

HOW DOES YOUR GARDEN GROW?

So, how do you grow plants in space? First, scientists have to figure out which plants are most "space-friendly." What does that mean? The best plants to send to space are fast-growing, don't need a lot of water, don't take up much room, provide lots of food, and are highly nutritious. Potatoes are a good example.

Astronaut Peggy Whitson (meet her on page 41!) shows off some healthy-looking soybean plants that have been grown hydroponically, with water and a nutrient solution, onboard the ISS.

Scientists also have to find new ways to grow plants in space. They've found that cultivating plants *hydroponically* (that means in nutrient-rich water, without dirt) works well in space. The hydroponic method actually speeds up plants' growth and uses less water than growing seeds in soil!

Astronaut Shannon Lucid checks on wheat plants growing on Russia's former space station, *Mir*.

GOOD ENOUGH TO EAT

Researchers have developed a new type of wheat for space, known as Apogee wheat, which is space-sized (shorter, so it takes up less space) and faster-growing, which means it can be harvested sooner than wheat on Earth. The wheat has been grown successfully in space using hydroponic methods and special lights to stand in for sunlight.

Scientists are developing other crops especially for space use, like short "super-dwarf" rice, soybean plants that grow extra quickly, and small pepper plants that produce big peppers!

Here you can see the space-sized "super-dwarf" rice, on the right, compared to the taller "semi-dwarf" rice on the left. Regular rice is even taller than both of these!

Pepper plants like these have been developed to be extra small—but their peppers are still big, which could make them great space food!

★Astrotales

Space Scent-sation!

One sweet discovery about plants in space is the fact that flowers don't smell the same as they do on Earth.

In 1998, a company called International Flavors and Fragrances sent a miniature rose plant into orbit on the space shuttle *Discovery*. The astronauts onboard collected samples of the flowers' oils and sent them home to be compared to oils from flowers down on Earth.

Scientists discovered that in weightlessness, the flowers released an aroma different from their normal scent on Earth! A team of scent experts was able to reproduce the smell of the oil sample chemically. Since then, the space scent has been used in two perfumes: Zen by Shiseido and Impulse by Unilever. Take a whiff if you see them in the store!

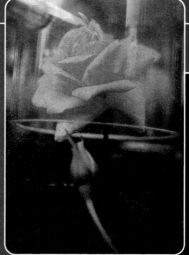

The rose plant in space...

...and back on Earth

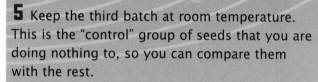

SEEDS
OF CHANGE

Being out in space means facing really harsh conditions, including extreme temperatures, radiation, and lack of air. Can seeds survive all that? Try this mission to see how they stand up to extreme heat and cold!

Launch Objective

> **Test whether exposure to extreme temperatures will prevent seeds from sprouting.**

Your equipment

▶ **Logbook and pencil**
▶ **Radish seeds** SPACE Case
▶ **Three aluminum pie tins or shallow ovenproof bowls**
▶ **Three cups (paper, plastic, or foam)**
▶ **Soil**
▶ **Water**
▶ **Marker**
▶ **Magnifier** SPACE Case

Personnel

▶ **An Intergalactic Adult (IGA)**

Mission Procedure

1 Predict what will happen to seeds that are exposed to heat and seeds that are exposed to cold. How do you think they'll grow compared to seeds left at room temperature? Write down your hypothesis in your logbook.

2 Count out thirty radish seeds and put ten in each pie tin or bowl.

3 Have an IGA place one batch in the oven for forty-five minutes at 250 degrees Fahrenheit (121 degrees C).

4 Place another batch in the freezer for one day.

5 Keep the third batch at room temperature. This is the "control" group of seeds that you are doing nothing to, so you can compare them with the rest.

6 Fill the three cups with soil. Label the cups OVEN, FREEZER, and CONTROL with your marker.

7 Moisten each cup with $\frac{1}{4}$ cup (60 ml) of water and add the right seeds to each cup, on top of the soil.

8 Set all three cups on a sunny windowsill and record the time and date in your logbook.

9 Check the seeds each day using your magnifier and record how many new sprouts you see from each group. Keep checking on your seeds for seven days and add enough water to keep the soil moist.

10 After a week, how many of the seeds in each batch have sprouted? Was your hypothesis correct?

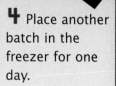
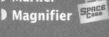

Science, Please!

You might have found that the frozen seeds sprouted first, followed by the control seeds, and then the heated seeds (which might not have sprouted at all).

Exposing seeds to cold temperatures can actually speed up their sprouting. That's because many species of seeds sprout after going through a cold period, like spending time in winter soil. By freezing the seeds, you're recreating that cold environment. On the other hand, heating a seed could damage the embryo inside and prevent it from sprouting.

If your results were different, can you think of reasons why? Try repeating your experiment to see if your results turn out the same!

More from Mission Control

1 Want to share your results with other scientist-cadets? Then hop on-line and head for this month's bulletin board at www.scholastic.com/space, where you can post and compare your findings!

2 Ready to design your own radical radish experiment? Then think of a question you want to answer and *grow* for it! What if you put several batches of seeds in the freezer, each for a different amount of time (a day, a week, two weeks)? Which batch do you think would sprout the fastest? Or what if you compared the growth of plants *outside* versus on the windowsill? Your fertile mind can sprout lots more ideas like these!

★Astrotales

You Say Tomato, I Say...

More than twelve million tomato seeds were sent into space in this compartment of the Long Duration Exposure Facility.

If seeds can still sprout after being exposed to freezing temperatures, what happens if they're exposed to the extreme environment of space?

Space scientists sent a whole bunch of tomato seeds into space in 1984 inside the Long Duration Exposure Facility along with over fifty other experiments. The seeds stayed in space for almost six years, where they were exposed to lack of air and water, radiation, and varying temperatures. They were then returned to scientists and students in schools across the United States, who planted the seeds and compared their growth to regular, Earth seeds.

As it turned out, space exposure didn't prevent the seeds from sprouting normally—and in fact, some experimenters found that the space seeds sprouted *faster* than the Earth ones! This could be good news for the future of plants in space! But scientists need to experiment more before they come to a conclusion.

Want to grow your own space seeds? Visit the Space U web site bulletin board to find out how *you* can participate in an experiment like this!

SEED RACER

So, cadet, do you have a "green thumb"? Are you good at growing plants? Well, never fear, because in this experiment, it won't be *your* fault if your plants don't thrive! You'll be testing different combinations of water and nutrients to see which plants grow well—and which ones don't!

Launch Objective

> **Compare the growth of plants in soil versus in water.**

Your equipment

- **Logbook and pencil**
- **Four cups (paper, plastic, or foam)**
- **Soil**
- **Distilled water (usually available at the grocery store in gallon jugs)**
- **Bottled spring water**
- **Radish seeds** SPACE Case
- **Cotton balls**
- **Marker**
- **Magnifier** SPACE Case

Mission Procedure

1 How do you think a plant grown hydroponically (in water) will compare to one grown in soil? And what kind of water do you think will help plants grow the most—spring water or distilled water? Write down your hypothesis in your logbook.

2 Fill your first cup with soil and moisten it with $\frac{1}{4}$ cup (60 ml) distilled water. Label this cup DISTILLED with your marker.

3 Fill your second cup with soil, moisten it with $\frac{1}{4}$ cup spring water, and label it SPRING.

4 Count out ten seeds for each cup and sprinkle them on the soil.

5 Fill the third and fourth cups with cotton that you've unraveled so it's thin and fluffy. This will allow the plants' roots to take hold.

6 Moisten the first cotton-filled cup with $\frac{1}{4}$ cup distilled water and label it DISTILLED.

7 Moisten the second cotton-filled cup with $\frac{1}{4}$ cup spring water and label it SPRING.

8 Sprinkle ten seeds into each of the cotton cups.

9 Place all four cups in a sunny window. Add either distilled or spring water every few days, only if the surface of the dirt or cotton is dry. Keep a record in your logbook of when you water each cup and how much water you add.

10 Study the seeds every day with your magnifier to check for new sprouts, and record your observations in your logbook.

11 After twelve days, which sprouts grew the tallest and look the healthiest? What did you find? Was your hypothesis correct? Be sure to write down your observations and your conclusion in your logbook!

Science, Please!

Plant seeds contain the nutrients the sprouts need for their first week or so of growth. After the first week, growth depends on factors such as sunshine, water, and minerals absorbed by the roots. In your experiment, all these variables were kept the same except the minerals absorbed by the roots—this was your variable. The minerals depended on which cup you planted your seeds in.

Distilled water does not have any minerals in it, so sprouts grown only in distilled water will reach a certain size and die. Spring water contains *some* but not *all* of the minerals that plants need. So the spring-watered plants might have lived longer or grown taller than the ones in distilled water, but they shouldn't have grown as well as the ones in soil.

The plants grown in soil got the minerals they needed from—you guessed it—the soil! Your soil-grown plants probably grew the same whether you added spring or distilled water. That's because the soil provided the nutrients the plants needed, so it didn't matter whether the water had additional minerals or not.

In order to grow plants successfully with the hydroponic method, you need to find just the right mix of minerals for the plant you're growing. Once that's figured out, hydroponically-grown plants can actually grow faster and better than ones grown in dirt. That's because roots soak up minerals more efficiently in water than in dirt. This is great news for space farming, because plants grown hydroponically can be squeezed into a smaller space than plants in soil. On a spacecraft, room is limited!

More from Mission Control

1 Because science in space isn't cheap, many space scientists "piggyback" one experiment with another. In other words, they may add another mini-experiment to one that's already being done. By sharing, you need fewer materials and less experiment time in space, which translates to serious savings!

So now that you've grown some plants, try out this piggyback experiment. Tuck a stack of folded newspaper halfway under one of the cups filled with dirt, so that it's tilted away from the window.

Observe what happens to the radish sprouts over a day. Write down your results in your logbook, and draw pictures to show what happens! Try tilting the cup in a different direction after a few days and observe again. What do you notice? Turn to page 48 to find out what our Space U sprout specialists discovered!

2 As with the previous mission, you can share your results on-line at www.scholastic.com/space!

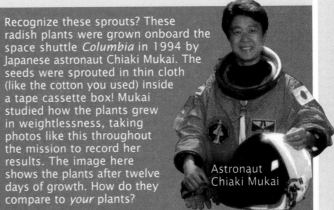

Recognize these sprouts? These radish plants were grown onboard the space shuttle *Columbia* in 1994 by Japanese astronaut Chiaki Mukai. The seeds were sprouted in thin cloth (like the cotton you used) inside a tape cassette box! Mukai studied how the plants grew in weightlessness, taking photos like this throughout the mission to record her results. The image here shows the plants after twelve days of growth. How do they compare to *your* plants?

Astronaut Chiaki Mukai

Part 3:
Animals in Space

IT'S A ZOO UP THERE!

Years before humans ever ventured beyond Earth, four-legged creatures were already exploring the space frontier. No, we're not talking about *aliens*, cadet! We're talking about dogs, monkeys, rats, and other furry space heroes who tested every aspect of space flight, making sure it was safe for people.

Today, all kinds of small animals and bugs are still sent onboard space shuttles and the ISS, where they live alongside astronauts. As pets? Not yet, cadet! By studying animals, scientists can better understand the changes that happen to living things (like us!) in weightlessness. This will help keep people healthy during long stays in space, and it might also help us learn more about our bodies down on Earth!

Sam, the monkey pictured here, was one of several animals sent onboard a spacecraft before humans went into space.

FLASH FACT

Animals that have been sent into space for research include fish, rats, snails, jellyfish, newts, frogs, tortoises, and more! Here, Astronaut Donald Thomas works with a newt onboard Spacelab.

DON'T TOUCH THE HUMANS!

Animals living onboard the space shuttle and the ISS are kept in special sealed cages, or habitats, designed to keep them comfortable in space and to make sure they're completely separated from the astronauts.

The animals are then monitored by cameras, sensors, and the crew members, too. The astronauts may be required to feed the animals, replenish their water supplies, or conduct tests—but they don't handle the animals directly or take them out of their habitats. Why not? Remember, these animals are experiments, not pets! Plus, astronauts don't want to risk being bitten, getting sick from animal germs, or having to clean up after any floating

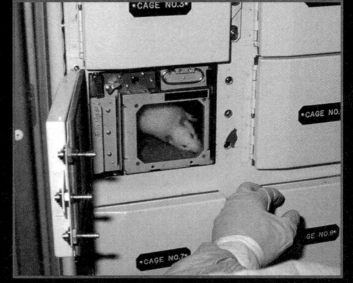

A rat in its habitat onboard Spacelab

messes the animals make—because you can't tell a rat to "hold it"! It's safer to keep animals inside their habitats or in a glovebox (you'll read more about gloveboxes on page 39).

FLASH FACT

In 1994, medaka fish (a species found in Asia) were sent into space onboard a space shuttle. While up in space, they were the first vertebrates (animals with a backbone) that mated successfully and had normal offspring!

WHAT HAVE WE LEARNED?

Scientists have discovered many interesting things by studying animals in space—like how they move around, sleep, eat, and lay eggs.

For example, male fruit flies sent into space don't live as long as they do on Earth—but females live just as long in space! And rats sent into space don't like being weightless, so they cling to each other or to the edges of their habitats instead of floating around! The more scientists learn about the way animals behave in space, the more they can understand things that affect humans in space, too.

FISH WAY'S UP?

Ever see a fish floating upside down? Yuck! We mean a fish that's *alive*, cadet! Well, in space, when fish don't know which way's up, they may swim upside down or sideways! Find out how fish figure out "what's up" by trying this mission!

Launch Objective

See how fish use light to orient themselves.

Your equipment

▶ Your scientific smarts!

Mission Procedure

How does a fish decide which way's up in weightlessness? Researchers in Japan wanted to test how fish use light for this purpose, so they set up the experiment you see below. A fish was placed inside a narrow tube so it didn't have room to swim around much, making it easier to study.

Researchers shined a light on one side of the fish, then switched it off and turned on a light on the other side. They then studied how the fish positioned itself depending on where the light was coming from.

1 Check out the fish pictured below. What do you think it will do when the light on the other side of its tube is turned on instead?

A) The fish will flip so that it's facing up instead of down.

B) The fish will turn its top toward the other light.

C) The fish will move as far away from the light as it can.

D) The fish will curl its tail in the direction of the light.

2 Choose a hypothesis from the list above and then turn to page 48 to see if your prediction is correct!

BUG OUT!

You've seen the way ants, spiders, and other creepy crawlies behave on Earth. Up in space, do you think they'd dig tunnels and spin webs like normal—or would they totally "bug out"?

Launch Objective

> Predict how bugs will behave in space!

Your equipment

▶ **Your insect instincts**
▶ **A pencil and paper**

Mission Procedure

Harvester ants are large ants that dig tunnels as deep as 15 feet (4.5 m) into the ground to hibernate during winter and to connect chambers for storing food, resting, and nursing their young.

In 2003, a group of high school students in New York sent specially-designed habitats containing harvester ants into space onboard a space shuttle. Although the ants usually tunnel through sand and dirt, the habitats contained a special gel made with seaweed extract that could withstand space travel and provide food for the ants. The students hypothesized that in space, the ants would tunnel less because they would be disoriented by weightlessness.

1 Take a look at the photo below of a harvester ant tunnel after thirteen days on Earth, in the same type of habitat that was sent into space. As you can see, the ants tunneled downward into the gel.

2 Now think about what you know about living things adapting to weightlessness and write a hypothesis predicting how ants living in the exact same habitat in space would tunnel, over the same period of time. Would they tunnel more, less, or the same? Would the tunnels be bigger, smaller, or the same size? Would they be in the same direction?

3 Now draw a picture of your tunnels, making them the way you think the ants would.

4 Turn to page 48 to see a photo of the ant habitat that was really sent into space, and check out its tunnels to see if your hypothesis was correct!

More from Mission Control

You've seen spiders spin their webs on Earth so they can catch their favorite flying snacks, right? Take a look at this ordinary Earth spiderweb and notice its features. Now, how do you think the same kind of spider would form a web in space?

A) It would not spin a web.

B) Its web would have a completely different shape and structure.

C) Its web would be bigger.

D) Its web would be less symmetrical.

Choose your hypothesis and draw the web as you imagine it will look. Then turn to page 48 to see a real web spun in space and find out if your prediction was right!

Part 4

People in Space

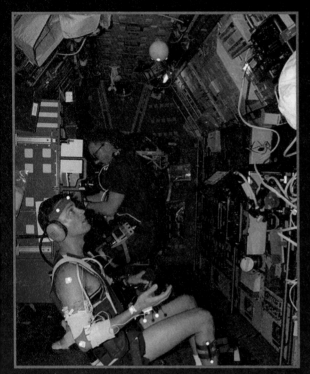

Astronaut Jim Pawelczyk practices catching a ball tossed at him by a device overhead, while sensors on his body detect how he reacts in weightlessness.

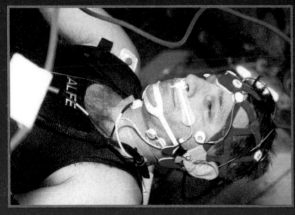

Astronaut Richard Linnehan is wearing a special cap that will measure electrical impulses from his brain, muscles, eyes, and heart while he sleeps.

Studying animals can help improve our understanding of what happens to our bodies in space. But the only way we'll ever *really* know what happens is by being there ourselves! That's why every astronaut who goes into space is essentially a human test subject. Astronauts collect blood and urine samples, hook their bodies up to machines that measure their heart performance, and use instruments that check their muscle mass. They even test their brain activity! That way, scientists back on Earth can carefully study every detail as they look for ways to keep people healthy in space.

OH, WHAT A FEELING!

We know that weightlessness has some pretty *heavy* effects on astronauts' bodies. When the blood pumped by the heart is no longer pulled down by the effects of gravity, it collects in the upper body, making the astronaut look and feel different. Muscles and bones weaken when they're not being used to support weight, and the brain gets confused when it can't tell up from down. And that's just to name a *few* changes.

Scientists study these and other changes by making careful measurements and keeping detailed logs. In the next few missions, you'll see what it's like to be a human test subject and learn about the changes astronauts go through up in space!

WHAT'S YOUR NORMAL?

Did you know that everyone's body has a different "normal"? It's true—each person's body has its very own normal temperature, blood pressure, weight, and so on. Try this mission to find *your* normal and see why it's important to know!

Launch Objective

> Determine what your "normal" is!

Your equipment

▶ Logbook and pencil
▶ Thermometer
▶ Piece of paper
▶ Tape
▶ Ruler
▶ Bathroom scale

Personnel

▶ Someone to help take measurements

Mission Procedure

1 Guess what your normal temperature, height, and weight will be throughout the day, and write down this hypothesis in your logbook.

2 Place a thermometer next to your bed before you go to sleep at night.

3 The next morning, take your temperature *before* you get out of bed. Record your temperature and the time in your logbook under the heading "morning."

4 After you get out of bed, stand against a wall on a floor with no carpet and tape a piece of paper to the wall at head level. Find a helper to put

a ruler flat on your head and mark your height on the paper on the wall.

5 Measure from the mark on the paper to the floor to see how tall you are. Write down your height under the "morning" heading in your logbook.

6 Wearing just your underwear, weigh yourself. Write this down, too.

7 In the middle of the day (after lunch or after school) repeat the three measurements, making sure to record them again. Just before bed, repeat them a final time.

8 Study your results. Are your measurements always the same?

Science, Please!

You should have found that your body measurements changed throughout the day.

You probably discovered that you were a little taller when you first woke up in the morning. That's because your spine wasn't compressed by gravity while you were lying in bed, so it stretched out a little. Gravity made you shorter by the end of the day.

You might have also found that your temperature was lower in the morning than during the day. That's because in the morning you were lying still, but during the day you were moving around, which raises your temperature. So, even though we say that 98.6 degrees Fahrenheit (37 degrees C) is "normal," your normal will be a range of temperatures that could be above or below this.

Finally, your weight may have changed a little depending on whether you'd just eaten or had a lot to drink.

Just like you did in this mission, astronauts collect their "normal" measurements on Earth (height, weight, temperature, blood pressure, and other vital signs). Then Mission Control can compare this range to measurements taken in space.

Here's what happens in space:

■ **Height:**

You know the spine-stretching you experienced in the morning? In weightlessness, with no pull of gravity, astronauts' spines stretch up to 3 to 4 inches (8 to 10 cm) taller!

■ **Temperature:**

Just like on Earth, this will vary depending on the astronaut's level of activity. Only temperatures outside the astronaut's normal range would cause concern.

■ **Weight:**

This can vary throughout the day for the same reasons it does on Earth. But astronauts also experience some loss in body mass while in space, partly because their bodies get rid of excess fluid (see page 29).

So, as long as the astronaut's "normal" Earth measurements have been established, we can get a good picture of the changes that go on in space!

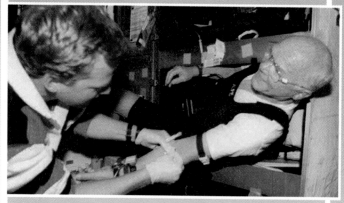

Astronaut John Glenn is preparing to have a blood sample drawn while onboard the space shuttle *Discovery*. In 1998, John Glenn was the oldest man to go into space, at age 77. Many tests were done on him to study the effects of space travel on his body.

★Astrotales

Finding NEEMO

What's another way scientists can learn about the effects of space on the human body—without actually sending anyone into space? By sending them underwater! That's right, cadet! NASA sends astronauts on NASA Extreme Environment Mission Operations (NEEMO), where crews practice space living in an undersea habitat known as "Aquarius" off the coast of Key Largo, Florida.

The NEEMO habitat is very similar in size to the modules of the ISS, and it's complete with its own Mission Control on shore! The astronauts live among the coral reefs and build things underwater to simulate space walks.

The fifth NEEMO mission was completed in June 2003. During the two-week mission, crew members studied the effect of their environment on sleep patterns. They also tested wireless medical equipment that would help Mission Control keep track of their health, and even tried out future space-walking gear!

B1RD

Did you know that astronauts get big heads in space? No, it's not because they think they're so great—their heads *actually* get bigger! They also get skinny legs, called "bird legs," because of the way their body fluids shift around in weightlessness. Try this mission to check out your own bird legs!

Launch Objective

▶ **See why astronauts get bird legs in space!**

Your equipment

▶ **Logbook and pencil**
▶ **Lined paper**
▶ **Scissors**
▶ **Chair**
▶ **Ruler**

Personnel

▶ **Friend to help take measurements**

Mission Procedure

1 What do you think will happen to the size of your ankles if you lie on the floor with your legs propped up? Write down your hypothesis in your logbook.

2 Cut two thin strips of lined paper across the length of the page so they have lines across them like a ruler.

3 Label one strip LEFT and the other RIGHT.

4 Sit on a chair and wrap the left strip around your left ankle at the narrowest part, just above your anklebone.

5 Mark the place where the edges of the paper overlap and label it SITTING. Repeat this for your right ankle.

6 Lie on the floor with both feet up on the chair for five minutes.

7 Now have your friend wrap the paper around each ankle while your feet are still up on the chair and make a new mark where the edges overlap. Label this mark LEGS UP.

8 With a ruler, measure the difference between the first mark and the second mark and record it in your logbook. What happened to your ankles? Did they change size? Was your hypothesis correct?

9 Make new strips of paper and try this mission again on your friend so you can compare your results! Remember, doing an experiment just once isn't enough to prove a theory!

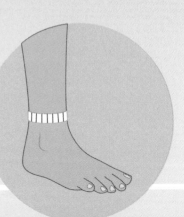

LEGS

Science, Please!

In this mission, you saw how lying down with your feet up made your ankles get smaller. When you're standing, gravity pulls the fluids in your body toward your legs. When you lie down, some of this fluid shifts toward your head, making your ankles skinnier.

In space, lots of body fluid remains in the upper body because it's not pulled down by gravity. This gives astronauts bigger heads and smaller legs than normal.

When an astronaut's brain senses all this extra fluid in the upper body, it thinks the whole body is overloaded with fluids, so it flushes out more fluid than usual through urination. This means that the astronaut has less total body fluid and even skinnier legs than yours were in this mission!

So what's the big deal about all these body-fluid changes? Well, when astronauts return to Earth, gravity pulls their body fluid back down into their legs. But since their bodies have less fluid than normal, their upper bodies don't have enough anymore! Without enough fluids in their heads, astronauts feel dizzy and could be in danger of fainting.

That's why astronauts drink lots of water before landing and eat salt tablets to help their bodies retain water. They also wear pressure suits that squeeze their legs, helping to push the fluids toward the upper body.

NASA is also experimenting with medicine to increase astronauts' blood pressure, which will help blood circulate throughout their bodies better. All this science will help astronauts adjust more quickly when they get back to Earth!

Astronaut Michael Foale is wearing the Lower Extremity Monitoring Suit, a pair of pants that has twenty sensors to measure the muscle and joint activity in his legs while he works onboard the ISS.

BRA1N

When astronauts go into space for the first time, it takes a while for them to adjust to weightlessness. But before long, they're zipping around without a problem. Try this mission to see what it's like to adjust to new surroundings!

Launch Objective

> See what happens when you confuse your brain.

Your equipment

▶ Brain Scramble Log pages
▶ Watch or timer
▶ Pencil
▶ Logbook
▶ Small mirror
▶ Thick hardcover book

Personnel

▶ Friend to time you

Mission Procedure

1 Visit www.scholastic.com/space and print out the Brain Scramble Log pages, where you'll find a copy of the maze you see on the right. If you don't have internet access, you can just complete the maze right here in the book.

2 Complete the maze normally while your friend times you. Pretty easy, right? Record your time in your logbook.

3 Now predict how long it will take you to complete the maze while you're looking at its mirror reflection. Write down your hypothesis in your logbook.

4 Erase your pencil lines and get ready for a real challenge!

5 With the maze on the table in front of you, prop up or hold your mirror behind it so you can see the maze reflected in the mirror.

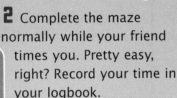

6 Stand a hardcover book on one end between you and the maze. The maze should be blocked from sight, but you should still be able to see it in the mirror by looking over the book.

7 While your friend times you, pick up your pencil, reach around the book, and complete your maze for the second time while looking at it only in the mirror (no peeking!). Write down your new time in your logbook.

8 How much longer did it take you to complete the maze using the mirror? Was your hypothesis correct?

9 If you printed out the Brain Scramble Log pages, try the other mazes and see if you can finish them faster than the first one. Does your brain get more comfortable working with the mirror reflection? If so, great! (Or should we say: ʇɐǝɹפ)

SCRAMBLE

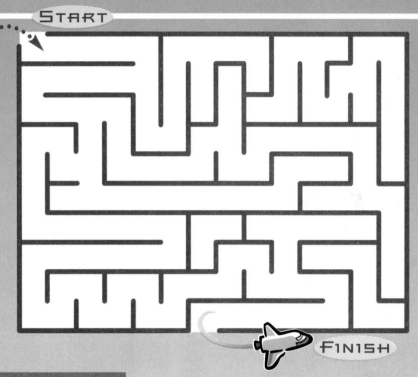

START

Can you help Astronaut Don B. Dizzy get to his spacecraft? It might seem simple at first— but try it while you're looking in a mirror!

FINISH

Science, Please!

Our brains depend on gravity to tell us how we're oriented. In our heads, it's actually our inner ear that tells us what's up and what's down. This is the *neurovestibular* system, and it tells your brain not only how you're oriented, but also how fast you're moving.

This mission was designed to give you an idea of how astronauts can get confused in space at first. Your body's usual sense of left, right, up, and down were all scrambled by looking in the mirror, so the maze took you much longer. In space, there isn't an up or down at all. Astronauts' brains get different signals than they're used to because they don't feel gravity, so they feel disoriented, sort of like you did while you were doing the maze in the mirror.

That's why it may take astronauts additional time to do things as their brains adapt to their new environment—just like it took more time for you to complete the maze using the mirror.

Some astronauts experience space sickness when they travel into space for the first time, because weightlessness is new to their bodies. Not only are their brains confused, but also, the fluid that's normally held in their legs collects in their upper bodies (as you learned in the previous mission). These two effects of weightlessness cause most first-time astronauts to feel sick. After a few days, their bodies become accustomed to weightlessness and adapt. Fortunately, their brains remember what they've learned, so space sickness isn't as big a problem on their next missions!

RADIATION ⚠ WORRIES

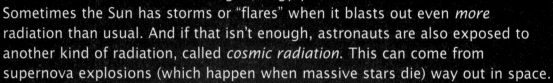

I n addition to stomach-turning stuff like space sickness and body changes like muscle and bone loss, astronauts face another health issue out in space: radiation.

Without the protection of the Earth's magnetic field, astronauts are directly exposed to the radiation pouring out of the Sun in the form of high-energy particles. Sometimes the Sun has storms or "flares" when it blasts out even *more* radiation than usual. And if that isn't enough, astronauts are also exposed to another kind of radiation, called *cosmic radiation*. This can come from supernova explosions (which happen when massive stars die) way out in space.

So what does all this add up to? Well, being exposed to radiation can cause hidden damage to human cells. This damage can show up later as cancer, eye problems like cataracts, and more. To protect astronauts' future health, if they reach a certain radiation dose, they're *grounded* (which means they can no longer fly on space missions). So far, no astronaut has been grounded.

Astronauts in orbit around Earth receive the largest doses of radiation on space walks, since they're no longer shielded by the walls of the spacecraft. However, scientists keep watch for solar flares and warn astronauts to stay inside when radiation levels are highest.

For trips beyond Earth orbit, spacecraft will have extra shielding and special "safe havens" where astronauts can go for even more protection during solar flares. And that's not all—researchers are also studying medications that astronauts can take to heal radiation damage in case they're accidentally exposed to too much. The more we know about radiation, the better we can plan for longer trips into space, to places like Mars—and beyond!

✶Astrotales

He's No Dummy!

F red was sent into space and lived on the ISS for four months to measure the amounts of radiation that astronauts are exposed to. Who is this guy? Well, he's a 3-foot (90-cm) tall, 95-pound (43-kg) dummy of a human body (with no arms or legs!). Inside Fred's fake plastic skin are fake organs and *real* human bones!

During his stay on the ISS, Fred was equipped with special detectors and sensors that read the level of high-energy particles that passed through his body. The information was then carefully analyzed to better understand exactly how much radiation is actually absorbed into the body, so that measures can be taken to protect astronauts better than ever.

SPACE SCIENCE ROCKS

The space environment makes some things trickier—like keeping muscles and bones healthy and growing plants—but it also makes other things easier and better than on Earth. Like what? A good example is growing crystals.

IN SPACE | ON EARTH

You can see a big difference in size here between the crystals grown in space and those from Earth.

Crystals are delicate things that have to be grown under the right conditions to be perfect. On Earth, gravity makes crystals grow squashed or clumped together. But in weightlessness, with nothing to squash them, crystals can grow much larger and be more perfectly shaped.

So what's the big deal about growing picture-perfect crystals? Well, for starters, many biological and medical mysteries could be solved if we better understood the structure of protein crystals. There are hundreds of thousands of proteins in the human body, but scientists still only understand a few of them.

By looking at floating, jumbo protein crystals grown in space, scientists can see things they wouldn't ordinarily be able to spot on Earth. They study the crystals with X rays and make computer images that break down their internal structures. Then they can use this information to understand the way our bodies react to diseases and drugs—which could lead to better medications to fight cancer, diabetes, and more.

In fact, super-sized space-grown crystals have already helped scientists understand the flu virus. With this new knowledge, they're developing drugs that will shorten the flu or help you avoid getting it in the first place!

IN SPACE | ON EARTH

Insulin crystals grown in space are much larger and clearer than those grown on Earth. Insulin is a protein created by the body. People with diabetes don't make enough, so they have to take doses of it.

In addition to super-crystals, scientists can also use the space environment to grow living human cells and tissue! On Earth, it's difficult to grow cells that look and behave like the ones in our bodies. It's also hard to get the cells to work together to form tissues. But in weightlessness, it's possible to grow really "life-like" cells and tissues, because the cells can be fooled into thinking they're floating inside a real human body.

For example, cancer cells grown in a weightless environment are 3-D (rather than flat, like cells grown on Earth) and closer to the size and shape of real cells in cancer patients. These space-grown cells can be used to study cancer and the medicines being developed to fight it.

Scientists have also been successful in growing human cartilage (tissue that connects bones) onboard the space station *Mir*. And, get this: They've also grown human heart tissue that actually *beats*. This real tissue can be used to test drugs and to better understand how a heart develops and functions. And perhaps it could be used one day to replace worn-out or damaged heart tissue. Imagine, cadet—spare body parts grown in space for Earthlings!

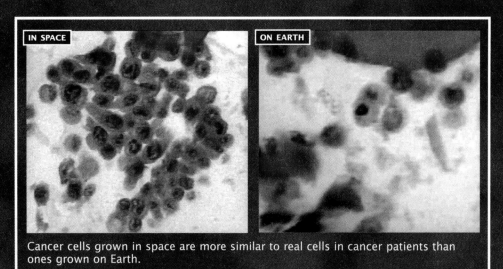

IN SPACE

ON EARTH

Cancer cells grown in space are more similar to real cells in cancer patients than ones grown on Earth.

Space is the place for learning more about diseases—and *also* for making medicines to fight them! Microcapsules are tiny drug capsules about the size of a human blood cell (in other words, very, very small!). They're better than regular medicines because they can be placed right where they're needed to fight disease without causing side effects to the rest of the body.

In weightlessness, bigger microcapsules that hold more medicine can be produced, since gravity doesn't deform them. That means that space is really the place to grow lifesaving stuff: protein crystals, human cells and tissues, *and* medicines!

CRYSTALS ROCK!

Ready to make your own homegrown crystals? Try this mission to create and compare two different kinds!

Grow different types of crystals and examine their structure and shape.

Your equipment

▶ **Two paper clips**
▶ **String** Space Case
▶ **Tall baby food or jam jar**
▶ **Microwave-safe measuring cup**
▶ **Water**
▶ **$\frac{1}{3}$ cup (80 ml) Epsom salts** Space Case
▶ **Food coloring**
▶ **Magnifier** Space Case
▶ **Logbook and pencil**
▶ **2 tablespoons sugar**
▶ **Shallow bowl**
▶ **Two wooden toothpicks**

Personnel

▶ **An Intergalactic Adult (IGA)**

Mission Procedure

Part 1: Epsom Salt Crystals

1 Tie a paper clip to your string and dangle it into a tall baby food jar or jam jar.

2 Unfold another paper clip and lay it across the mouth of the jar. Tie the other end of the string to it, so the first paper clip dangles down into the jar. Then set the string and paper clips aside.

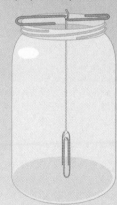

3 Have your IGA pour $\frac{1}{3}$ cup (80 ml) of boiling water into a measuring cup.

4 Then have your IGA add $\frac{1}{3}$ cup of Epsom salts and stir until most of the crystals have dissolved and the water looks clear.

5 To make it easier to see your crystals, you can put one drop of food coloring into the mixture and stir. Then pour the mixture into your jar.

6 Hang the string back down into the jar.

7 After the jar has cooled for at least fifteen minutes, put it in the refrigerator.

8 Without moving the crystals, use your magnifier to take note of the size and shape of the crystals after two to three hours. Write the details down in your logbook.

9 Take another peek after four to five hours, and then again the next day. Most crystals will probably form at the bottom of the jar because of the pull of gravity, but some should form on the string and the paper clip.

10 After twenty-four hours, remove the string carefully from the jar and examine the crystals once more. Take notes on what you see! What are your crystals shaped like? How big are the biggest ones?

Part 2: Sugar Crystals

1 In your logbook, write down a hypothesis predicting what you think sugar crystals will look like compared to the Epsom salts crystals. Do you think they'll be the same shape?

2 Have your IGA pour $\frac{1}{4}$ cup (60 ml) of boiling water into a measuring cup.

3 Then have your IGA add 2 tablespoons of sugar and stir for at least a minute.

4 Pour the mixture into a shallow bowl and set it on a counter where it won't be disturbed.

5 Float two wooden toothpicks on top of the water/sugar mixture.

6 Check the mixture with your magnifying glass an hour later. You may see a sparkly "ice" layer on top.

7 Twenty-four hours later, pick up one of the toothpicks and examine the crystals with your magnifier. What do they look like? Take notes on what you see.

8 If you like, you can leave the mixture on the counter for several days and it will continue to form crystals. Sugar crystals are also known as rock candy—so eat it up and enjoy!

Science, Please!

Crystals are made up of molecules that connect together into a solid shape. As you've seen by looking at your crystals up close, a pattern repeats over and over again throughout their structure.

The Epsom salts and sugar you used to make your crystals were *already* crystals when you began—they were just a lot *smaller*. By dissolving the crystals in water, you separated the molecules so they could reconnect and form bigger shapes when the water evaporated. Since each ingredient you used (Epsom salts or sugar) is made up of different molecules, you ended up with very different-looking crystals.

Inside *you*, your cells are constantly creating teeny-tiny protein molecules that build, support, and run your body. Protein molecules can be made into crystals, just like the crystals you grew. And just like your crystals, protein crystals come in all different shapes. The more scientists understand the shapes of protein crystals, the more they can learn about the protein molecules that make them up—and how the proteins work to keep our bodies running smoothly!

These different types of protein crystals grown in space all have different shapes.

More from Mission Control

Try adjusting your crystal-growing procedure and see how your results change. Try varying the amount of sugar, Epsom salts, or water you use. Or, see what happens if you let your crystals cool on a sunny windowsill compared to in the refrigerator. What other variables can you work with?

IT'S CRYSTAL CLEAR

How does gravity cause problems when you grow crystals on Earth? Compare your Earth-grown crystals to space-grown ones and find out!

Launch Objective

Grow your own salt crystals and compare them to ones grown in space!

Your equipment

▶ **Logbook and pencil**
▶ **Shallow bowl**
▶ **Water**
▶ **1 teaspoon salt**
▶ **Two wooden toothpicks**
▶ **Magnifier**

Mission Procedure

1 How will the salt crystals you grow compare to salt crystals grown in space? Write down your hypothesis in your logbook.

2 Pour 2 tablespoons of hot tap water into a shallow bowl.

3 Add 1 teaspoon of salt and stir the water for at least a minute, until almost all the grains of salt are dissolved and no longer visible.

4 Float two wooden toothpicks in the water, and set the bowl on a sunny windowsill or a warm place where it won't be disturbed.

5 Check the mixture with your magnifier four hours later. Do you see any salt crystals forming? How big are they now? Do they form regular shapes that you can draw? Try sketching them in your logbook!

6 Twenty-four hours later, pick up one of the toothpicks and examine the crystals with your magnifier.

7 Turn the page and compare your crystals to the ones grown in space. Write down the differences you see in your logbook!

Science, Please!

The biggest crystal in the photo below is over ¼ inch (6 mm) across. How wide was *your* biggest?

You might have noticed that as your crystals grew, the biggest ones fell to the bottom because they were heavy, and more crystals piled on top of them. That makes the crystals hard to see clearly and study. But in weightlessness, this isn't a problem!

Notice how the biggest crystal in this image is mostly by itself, not clumped to many other crystals? That's because it formed while floating in water—not piled together with other crystals at the bottom of a bowl.

These crystals (shown magnified) were grown onboard the ISS during Expedition 6 in 2003.

Do your salt crystals have a similar structure?

¼ inch (6 mm)

ACTUAL SIZE

HANDS-ON SCIENCE

Because of the sheer numbers of experiments that go into space, many of them are run remotely by Mission Control. Video cameras record the experiments so that scientists back on Earth can see what's going on and the astronauts onboard don't have to spend precious time on them. At other times, it's essential for astronauts to work on experiments with their own hands! Often, this calls for a glovebox.

A scientific glovebox is something you find in many laboratories on Earth. It's basically a sealed box with gloves attached to it. Scientists can stick their hands into the gloves and handle what's inside the box without contaminating it, or *getting* contaminated themselves!

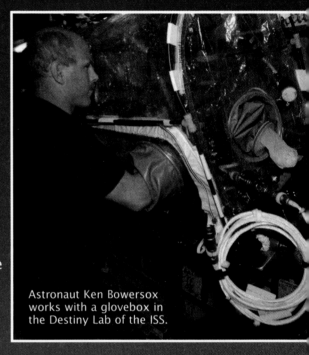

Astronaut Ken Bowersox works with a glovebox in the Destiny Lab of the ISS.

GLOVEBOXES IN SPACE

Gloveboxes are especially *handy* when it comes to dealing with hazardous materials. In weightlessness, even a blob of water can become a hazard if it's floating around near an instrument panel. That's why the glovebox was sent into space: so that crew members could do experiments involving liquids, fumes, flames, and animals without risking harm to themselves or their spacecraft.

Astronaut Pedro Duque works with a crystal-growing experiment in a glovebox on the ISS.

Onboard the ISS, the glovebox is called the Microgravity Science Glovebox, or MSG for short. Astronauts can see into the box through plastic windows and handle things with the built-in gloves. There's also a video camera attached, so that scientists back on Earth can watch experiments as they take place in orbit. When astronauts need to handle animals onboard, they can slide their habitat into the box and then work with them using the gloves. The first glovebox experiment done on the space station involved melting semiconductor crystals, which could lead to better and faster computer chips!

BALLOON BLOW-UP

> You normally think of wind as moving something—like your hair, leaves, or flags, right? Did you know that blowing air can *also* hold something in place? Try this mission to see how!

Launch Objective

> See how air can be used to keep objects in place in space.

Your equipment

▶ One or two round balloons
▶ Hair dryer

Personnel

▶ A friend to give you a hand

Mission Procedure

1 Blow up your balloon and tie it shut.

2 Plug in your hair dryer and point it up. Ask your friend to hold the balloon over the hair dryer.

3 Turn on the hair dryer, starting with the lowest setting first, and see what happens to the balloon.

4 Try higher hair dryer settings. Does the balloon stay in place or fly away?

5 Try adding a second balloon below the first. Can you keep both balloons in place above the hair dryer?

Science, Please!

In this mission, you used blowing air from a hair dryer to hold a balloon in place. In space, when scientists want to keep an experiment from floating away while they're working on it, they can use not only wind, but also magnetism and even sound waves!

In your case, you were able to keep the balloon in place with air blowing only from below. That's because the force of gravity was pushing down on the balloon to balance the force of the wind pushing up. In space, the balloon would just float up, up, and away if you tried this! You'd need to also have air coming from above to hold the balloon in place.

This technique can be used in space to melt metals to make alloys (metal mixtures) without using a container! This is great because when alloys are made inside a container, some of the container can melt into the mixture and contaminate it. In space, using this technique (which is called *containerless processing*), astronauts can make super-pure alloys!

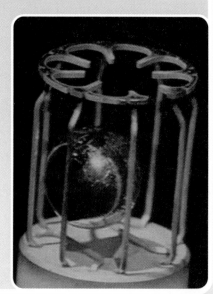

The metal ball here, which is about $\frac{2}{5}$ of an inch (1 cm) across, was created onboard Spacelab using containerless processing. It was suspended inside the cage using magnetism while the metal melted and cooled.

Peggy Whitson

ASTRONAUT

Peggy Whitson was named the first NASA Science Officer during her stay onboard the ISS in 2002. She spent six months on the ISS, where she completed twenty-one scientific investigations, including studies on the human body in weightlessness.

She was also responsible for activating and checking out the Microgravity Science Glovebox, which gave her a hands-on feel for science in space!

Question: How did you practice and prepare on Earth to do experiments up in space?

Answer: We have training facilities here to practice setting up the experiments. We even conduct simulations in which we perform the experiments while talking with the ground team and asking them questions.

Q: What types of experiments did you enjoy working on most during your stay on the ISS?

A: All types of experiments were interesting—everything from soybeans to superconductors!

Q: What was the coolest thing about doing experiments in space?

A: Even after months of being in orbit, I still marveled that I was actually conducting science in an orbiting laboratory, 220 miles (350 km) above the Earth!

Q: Did you ever use a glovebox? What did you do with it?

A: We did a number of experiments looking at how superconductor crystals formed. The components were melted at temperatures as high as 835 degrees Fahrenheit (446 degrees C)!

Q: Did you perform any experiments on your own body?

A: We looked at our lung function before and after space walks, since there is a difference in the pressure of the station (which is like sea level here on Earth) and the pressure in the suit (which is slightly lower to make the suit less stiff). We also looked at the strength and density of our bones before and after space flight.

Q: What is the most important thing for kids to know about science in space?

A: Science in space provides a very unique environment to determine how physical, chemical, and biological processes change in weightlessness. There's no place here on Earth that can provide the same environment.

Q: If you could go back into space and only do one experiment up there, what would it be?

A: The experiment that required that I spend the most time in orbit!

Here, Peggy Whitson works with the Microgravity Science Glovebox in the Destiny Lab on the ISS.

Part 6:
Space Spin-Offs

Did you know that the science that's done in space actually touches your life on Earth every day? Whether you're at home, at school, or at the mall, you're probably benefiting from something that was created from research done in or for space. How does that happen? Through space spin-offs—products that apply space technology to Earth!

What types of spin-offs are we talking about here? Here's a short list of some of them to give you an idea of how space science fits into your life!

NO SMOKING!

Your home is probably protected by a smoke detector, right? Well, that's a lifesaving device we owe to NASA! NASA developed a smoke and fire detector for its first space station, *Skylab*, back in the 1970s, which would alert astronauts to harmful vapors. It was adapted into the modern-day smoke detector you find in your home, at school, at restaurants, and around town!

CHECK OUT THESE CODES

Can you imagine having the job of keeping track of the millions of parts that go into making a spacecraft? That's why the brains at NASA developed the bar-code system, to keep their inventory in order. Bar codes are now found all over the place—on products you buy in stores, on library books, and more. These patterns of thick and thin black lines might look meaningless to *human* eyes, but computers can scan them and find out prices and other information in a snap!

CORDLESS WONDERS

Ever reach for a cordless hand vacuum to take care of a spill? Cordless tools are pretty handy for getting jobs done on Earth when you're not near an electrical outlet or don't want to get tangled up in cords. But just imagine how far you'd be from an outlet if you were on the Moon! That's why the first portable power tools were created for Apollo astronauts to drill for Moon samples. This technology was later used to make a bunch of other power tools, like hand vacuums, shrub trimmers, grass shears, and more!

OPEN UP AND SAY "WOW!"

Ever see an ear thermometer? These gadgets measure your temperature using an infrared sensor (a *heat* sensor) that goes into your ear for only two seconds. It sure beats having to hold a thermometer in your mouth for a whole minute! NASA developed this amazing tool with the same technology they use to measure the temperatures of stars and planets from here on Earth!

NO MORE METAL MOUTH

Ever see "invisible" braces on someone's teeth—the kind with clear brackets instead of metal ones? These brackets are made of the same kind of ceramic material NASA is developing for spacecraft. Ceramics can stand up to super-hot temperatures, so they're great protection for the outside of a spacecraft. And the same stuff looks great on your teeth, too!

MADE FOR THE SHADE

During the 1980s, NASA's Jet Propulsion Laboratory researched material that filters out harmful light. That research led to the development of special lenses for sunglasses that block out the Sun's harmful ultraviolet light. NASA also came up with scratch-resistant coating while working on how to protect spacecraft from the harsh environments they face. This coating can now be found on the lenses of sunglasses, too!

SO HOT, IT'S COOL

Laser technology designed to study the Earth's atmosphere is now close to many people's hearts. In fact, it's helping to keep their hearts working right! Laser surgery was never possible on the heart because lasers were too hot for delicate heart tissue. But now, through NASA laser technology, there's a new type of laser that stays cool enough to use for heart surgery!

KEEP ON SPINNING

So, does that quick list of spin-offs sound like a lot, cadet? Well, that's just the beginning! Space science has also been used to develop all of these things, too:

■ **Breathing systems for firefighters**

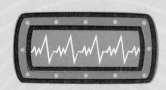

■ **Super-insulating blankets for survival in cold conditions**

■ **Special foam mattress material that shapes itself to the sleeper's body**

■ **Racing swimsuits with ribbed fabric to help swimmers move faster through water**

■ **Improved solar power systems**

■ **Heart monitors**

■ **Robot-guided wheelchairs**

■ **Flat-screen televisions**

■ **Joysticks for video games, and much, much more!**

THE WRITE STUFF!

Does an ordinary ballpoint pen have the *write stuff* to make it in space? Or does it need to be specially designed for the space environment? Try this mission to find out!

Launch Objective

▷ **Find out how a ballpoint pen would work in space!**

Your equipment

▷ **Ballpoint pen**
▷ **Two sheets of paper**
▷ **Hardcover book**

Mission Procedure

1 Find a ballpoint pen that has thick ink, not wet ink that smears. Choose a new pen if you can—or at least one that's not old and about to run out of ink. Test it out with a few scribbles to make sure it's working okay.

2 Label one sheet of paper UPSIDE DOWN and lay it on top of a hardcover book.

3 Holding the paper and book upside down over your head, write your name (or any word you want) as many times as you can before your ink runs out. How many times could you do it?

4 Make a few scribbles holding the pen right side up until it writes well again.

5 Now try holding your paper vertically. Label another sheet VERTICAL and again try writing your name or word many times, making sure you're holding the pen with the ink tip slightly above the end. Could you write longer with your pen in this position? How long until your ink stopped running *this* time?

6 If possible, open up your pen and have a look at its insides. Can you figure out why the ink wouldn't flow well when you wrote upside down and vertically? How well do you think your pen would work in space?

Science, Please!

Your ballpoint pen should have stopped working pretty quickly when you were writing upside down. You might have had a bit more luck writing vertically, depending on how you angled your pen. The more "upside down" you tilted the pen, the more quickly the ink should have stopped flowing.

This happens because ballpoint pens use gravity to pull the ink down to the tip. The pen has to be angled downward for gravity to do its job—otherwise, you're out of luck!

If you figured out that this kind of pen would not work well in space, you're *write* on! Just like when you turned the pen upside down, the ink wouldn't flow out of the tip in the weightlessness of space.

Can you think of ways you could modify the pen's design so it would work in space? Check out the Astrotale below to find out how one inventor did just that!

The ink is thick enough that it won't flow out the open end of the tube when you hold the pen upside down.

Ink tube (open at end)

★Astrotales

The Space Pen

If ballpoint pens can't handle writing upside down, then how can they be made to work in the weightlessness of space?

Paul Fisher solved the problem in the 1950s when he designed a special refill ink cartridge for ballpoint pens. As you just saw in the mission above, normal ballpoint pen cartridges have to be used right side up, so that gravity can pull the ink down through the pen and onto your paper. The cartridges are open at the top end, allowing air to get inside as the ink flows out.

Fisher designed his refill ink cartridge in a new way—with no opening at the top! Instead, the ink was sealed inside a pressurized chamber, which meant that the ink was always being pushed toward the pen tip—whether you were writing up, down, or sideways! To keep the ink from flowing out the tip of the pen when it wasn't being used, Fisher used a special, thick kind of ink that wouldn't come out until you started writing.

Because it doesn't need gravity to work, the Fisher space pen was used on all the Apollo missions, and it's currently used for all manned space flights. It also serves well for the United States Air Force, undersea explorers, ski teams, and mountain climbers!

Wondering why astronauts don't just use a *pencil*? Well, they certainly could. But pencil markings will fade over time, which means astronauts could lose important information. Ink, on the other hand, stays put!

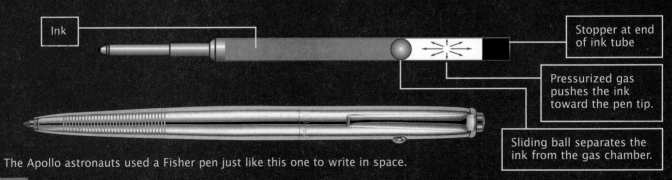

Ink

Stopper at end of ink tube

Pressurized gas pushes the ink toward the pen tip.

Sliding ball separates the ink from the gas chamber.

The Apollo astronauts used a Fisher pen just like this one to write in space.

It's Safe to Conclude

So, cadet, did you predict that your adventures in out-of-this-world science would be packed with cool discoveries? Then hopefully it's safe to conclude that your hypothesis was correct!

This month, you saw the science that researchers have taken into orbit—everything from growing space-age vegetables to finding clues to cure diseases back on Earth. You learned how some of the amazing technology developed for space has come back to our planet to change our lives forever. *And* you got a handle on the scientific method with several special science missions of your own! Way to go!

So, what's in store *next* month at Space U? A 3-D tour around Mars? A journey into a black hole? Something else? Make your prediction and check your mailbox next month to see if your "hypothesis" comes true!

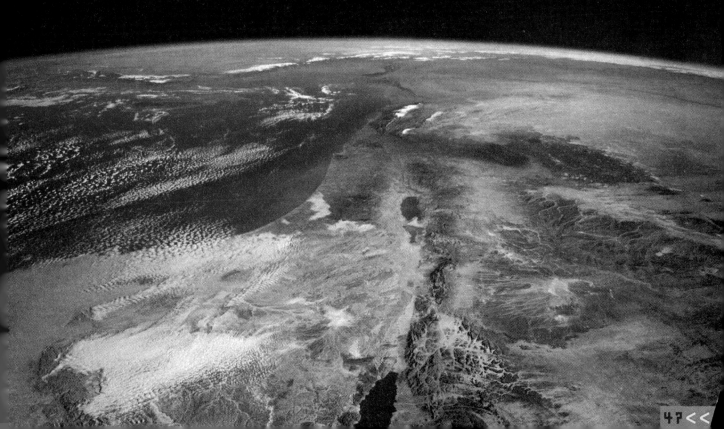

THE ANSWER STATION

Page 20: **Seed Racer**

The plants should grow toward their light source, as shown here.

In space, light may not always be coming from above, like on Earth, where plants rely on the Sun. That means that in space, plants could grow sideways, or even upside down!

Page 23: **Fish Way's Up?**

Here's what the fish did when the other light was turned on:

So, hypothesis **B** turned out to be correct.

Why? On Earth, fish know which way is up because of gravity, but they also get used to light coming from the Sun above them.

In space, where fish can't feel gravity, they point the tops of their bodies toward a light source, just like the fish pictured here. They can also use plants to orient themselves. In weightlessness, fish get confused, swim round and round, and even collide into the sides of their tanks. This is space sickness fish-style! And like astronauts, it takes a few days for the fish to adjust to their new surroundings. Having a similar setup to what they're used to on Earth while in space could help the fish adapt sooner.

Several studies have been done on fish in space. One concluded that the fish that adjust quickest to a space environment have better eyesight than others. This could mean that astronauts with extra-sensitive eyes may fare best in space!

Page 24: **Bug Out!**

Here's what the ants' tunnels looked like after thirteen days in space:

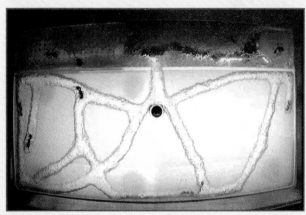

Wow! The students discovered that the ants in space tunneled like crazy, far more than the control group of ants on the ground. They concluded that this may have been because it's so much easier to move in weightlessness.

Below you'll find the results of the **More from Mission Control** experiment. As you can see, this space-made web is pretty similar to the webs spiders make on Earth, although it's not as perfectly symmetrical (so hypothesis **D** was the correct one). This could mean that, like humans, spiders can be a bit disoriented in weightlessness. But the next web the spider built was better than the first! Experiments with all these animals show that they can adapt and survive in weightlessness, just like humans.

Notice how the web is much more built-up on this side.